I Have
FALLEN

But Jesus...

Dr. Cassundra White-Elliott

This book is a work of non-fiction. However, specific names of individuals and the details of each incident have been changed and/or slightly altered to protect identities.

Bible scriptures are from the King James Version of the Bible, unless where otherwise noted.

CLF Publishing, LLC.
9161 Sierra Ave, Ste. 203C
Fontana, CA 92335
www.clfpublishing.org

ISBN # 978-0-9960815-9-7

Printed in the United States of America.

Dedications

This book is dedicated to everyone who has ever made a misstep and fallen into sin. Romans 3:23 says, *"For all have sinned, and come short of the glory of God."* God is a loving and a forgiving god. Go to Him and make amends. Don't worry about man. Man has no heaven or hell to put you in. But, you can return to the loving arms of the Lord, and He will make it all well again.

Acknowledgements

I acknowledge my heavenly father for placing this project on my heart. I know that my living is not in vain as long as I do what He directs me to do. For, He knows what His people need.

Introduction

Each and every day of our lives presents a new adventure, a new twist, and/or a new turn. Sometimes, the adventure will lead us exactly where we expect or desire to be. While at other times, we may end up somewhere we never desired or thought we would be. Sometimes, we make calculated moves, while other times our moves are quite by happenstance or accident.

Some of the moments we experience will be pain free, carefree and joyful. Other moments will be full of pain and/or filled with tears. We may even experience restless or sleepless nights. But all in all, whatever life brings our way, as believers, we serve a god who is more than able to keep us or get us back on the right track, if we have a heart to do so.

What we must understand is- we are human, clothed in flesh and blood, born in sin and shaped in iniquity. But simply because we are flesh, blood, and bones and have a sin nature, does that mean we cannot walk upright before the Lord? God expects us to live a sin-free life. Does that mean that we will not fall short? What does it all mean?

The word of God says a righteous man falls seven times. What that tells us is even a man who has been made righteous through Christ can fall. He may have a heart that is filled with love for God and a mind to do what is right, but at times he may fall short. This is why Jesus came, shed His blood and died on the cross, so we can have a way back to the Father.

The purpose of this book is to reassure you that if you have fallen by the wayside, or if you have engaged in an activity that is not pleasing to God, there is still hope for you. God still loves you! Remember, *"Be strong and of a good courage, fear not, nor be afraid of them: for the LORD thy God, he it is that doth go with thee; he will not fail thee, nor forsake thee,"* (Deuteronomy 31:6).

What the enemy wants to do is lead you onto a path of torture, a path of regret, and a path of shame. He wants to berate you and constantly remind you of the act you committed. But, God wants you to come to Him to right your wrong. He wants you to come to Him, so He can cleanse you of your sins and throw them into the Sea of Forgetfulness. He wants you to turn around and get back on the path of the straight and narrow.

God's word says in II Chronicles 7:14, *"If my people, which are called by my name, shall humble themselves, and pray, and seek my face, and turn from their wicked ways; then will I hear from heaven, and will forgive their sin, and will heal their land."*

The verse begins with three simple words, "If my people." 'If' is the first part of a condition. 'My people' refers to the children of God, those who have accepted Jesus Christ as their personal lord and savior. So, the verse states, if those who are called by God's name will humble themselves, pray, seek God's face, and turn from their wicked ways, then He will hear from heaven and heal their land.

The message in this verse is for the people of the world, the sinners. It is for the people of God who love God with all their heart but have fallen into temptation or some type of wickedness. But, God loves us so much that He will make a way of escape for us, so we can flee from the temptation (I Corinthians 10:13).

Even with the way made clear to escape evildoings, some have chosen not to take the way of escape. Some may have not even realized the way was there for them because Satan blinded their eyes with the snares he set before them.

But, even if you didn't escape through the way provided by the Lord and have found yourself entangled in sin, it is not too late to get back on track and to make things right with God.

If you are reading this book or someone is reading it to you, you have life in your body and you have air in your lungs. If you can read or listen, you can speak (or at least think). Therefore, you can repent before the Lord with the assurance that He will accept you with open arms. All you need to do is cry out to Him. He is guaranteed to receive you!

If you are not yet convinced God will receive you back, read the following accounts, and you will see for yourself that He will do just that!

Scared Straight

*"Lest Satan should get an advantage of us:
for we are not ignorant of his devices."*

II Corinthians 2:11

Dominic and Alexis have been married for twelve years. They have their share of ups and downs, just like any other married couple. But together, they are fearless. When you see one, you see the other. Over time, they have come to be known as 'The DA,' which, of course, is short for Dominic and Alexis.

In their relationship, they have what some would call role reversals. Dominic, although he is a man, is more of the talkative one, while Alexis is accustomed to holding her innermost feelings inside. She gives a whole new meaning to having a wall up. During her childhood, she learned to hold her thoughts and feelings in rather than share them freely with others. She was taught to keep personal things personal.

Dominic's upbringing, on the other hand, was completely different. When his family sat down for dinner, which they did each and every night, each family member shared the events of his/her day. As a result of those experiences, Dominic is an open book. Sharing his thoughts and feelings is second nature.

Month by month and year by year, Dominic had a strong desire for intimate conversations with his wife. But more and more often, she would be busy in her study and would not engage in in-depth conversations with him.

One day, quite unexpectedly, Dominic received a call from an old friend whom he once dated fifteen years ago. He was happy to hear his friend's voice, for he knew she was always someone who would lend a listening ear. Although it had been fifteen years since they dated, they spoke every couple of years or so to check in with each other, but the calls would always be discontinued after a few weeks.

When he first received the call, Dominic and his friend Kim would talk once or twice a week, but as time passed, instead of the calls decreasing, they began to converse twice a week and then every day. Sometimes, they spoke even two to three times a day. Dominic was pleased to finally have someone to listen to him when he wanted to vent or to just shoot the breeze.

During the course of time that Dominic would call Kim and receive her calls, he still tried to reach out to his wife because he was dedicated to her, and he did not want anyone or anything to interrupt his relationship with her. At the same time, he was not oblivious to Kim's desires pertaining to him. He knew deep down she always wanted more than just a friendship with him. However, he did not feel the same way, for he was committed to his wife and had vowed to keep their relationship holy and sanctified.

As time went on and the conversations continued, Kim and Dominic decided to meet for lunch. They enjoyed seeing each other and sharing time together. When Kim saw Dominic, her heart skipped a beat. When Dominic saw Kim, he saw a good friend and felt nothing but agape love for her.

As the months passed and the conversations continued, Dominic and Kim continued to meet for lunch about once a month. After lunch, they would always go their separate ways.

Little by little, Kim began to offer things to Dominic that Alexis had not been offering, such as a listening ear, advice, feedback on challenging situations, and even cooked meals. It wasn't that Alexis did not cook. She just didn't do it as often as Dominic desired.

Conveniently, Kim did not live too far from Dominic and Alexis, so from time to time when she had leftovers from the dinner she had cooked the night before, she would offer for Dominic to stop by and pick up a lunch on his way to work. When Dominic arrived, Kim would be standing just outside the parking area to hand him his neatly packed lunch. He would say a quick hello, without getting out of the car, and continue on his way to work.

One day when Dominic stopped by Kim's apartment to pick up the lunch she had prepared for him, he did not find her standing outside with his lunch bag ready to go. Reluctantly, he found a place to park and walked over to her door and knocked on it. When Kim opened the door,

Dominique found her very scantily dressed. What she had on left nothing to the imagination.

He immediately became sexually aroused; however, his willpower kicked in, and he told her he could not stay because he needed to get to work right away.

For the rest of that day and the days to follow, Dominic could not get the vision of Kim's sensual body out of his mind. He began to recall the intimate times they had spent together years ago. And every time he heard her voice, the image of her would appear right before his eyes.

About two weeks later, Kim invited Dominic over again. That time, he cleared his schedule, but in the back of his mind, he was holding tight to his commitment to his wife. As he walked through the doorway, once again he found Kim very provocatively dressed, and once again, he was aroused.

As they were not strangers and had been intimate before, Kim knew exactly what to do to push his buttons. She had heard what he said about being committed to his wife, but she knew what a good man he was, and she really desired him for herself. At the same time, it wasn't her desire to break up a marriage or a happy home. But for some reason, she could not ignore her own desires for Dominic.

When he walked in, he very casually sat on the couch in her living room. He did not want to expose his arousal to Kim. He figured by sitting down, he could camouflage it. But, Kim had a mind of her own. She walked over and sat next to Dominique on the couch with one leg up, exposing her red lace panties. When Dominique looked down, he noticed the moisture between her legs seeping through her panties. His arousal deepened, and he could no longer hide his reaction.

Kim calmly slid one leg across his lap and pulled her body on top of his, causing her to face him as she sat on his lap. Slowly, she lowered her head and placed her thick, succulent lips onto his and began to kiss him passionately. Dominic did not resist. He let his physical urges overtake him.

Before he knew it, Kim had unbuttoned his pants, removed her red lace panties, and had mounted him. All Dominic knew was the warm moisture of her body that surrounded his body was more than he could handle. In the back of his mind, he thought about Alexis, and then he thought about Kim, and then he thought about Alexis again, and he asked himself what he was doing there and how it even got to that point. But, then he thought about Kim again and what she was doing to him. Her firm legs lifted her body up and down, and he began to be lost in the moment.

At that point, his thoughts of Alexis faded out, and all he could focus on was what Kim was doing to him. As she continued to move and squeeze her muscles tightly, he felt himself explode inside of her. It was at that moment, he realized he had not protected himself from anything she may have transmitted to him or even to prevent pregnancy from occurring.

Immediately, Dominic lifted Kim off him, and he went to the restroom to clean himself up. With a guilty conscious, Dominic said his goodbyes and quickly left Kim's apartment. He was unable to look her in the eyes.

Over and over again as he drove home, he asked himself, *Why did I do that? How did I allow myself to get into this situation?*

I never want to hurt my wife. I never want to disappoint God. What if I contracted something from her and pass it over to my wife? What if Kim gets pregnant?

Finally, it killed him to think about the god he serves each and every day of his life, the god he committed his life to, the one he committed his service to. He knew God was looking down on him, and he knew God was not pleased. More than anything, that bothered him deeply.

When he got into his car, he shed a few tears. He felt like such a disappointment and a failure in the sight of God. He wondered what Alexis would do if she ever learned of his indiscretion. He really didn't know what had driven him to commit such an atrocious act. He knew no matter what his wife did or didn't do, there was no excuse for the act he had just committed.

After leaving Kim's apartment, Dominic made his way to work, but he was unable to perform the required duties. All he could think about was the sin he had committed. Through all of his thoughts, he could not forget God is a loving and a forgiving God. But, he also knew that God holds those who are called to ministry to a higher standard, and he was an elder in the church.

The last thing Dominic wanted to do was to be displeasing to God and to be that foul smelling odor unto God's nostrils. Instead, he wanted to be a sweet smelling savor unto God by being an honorable man. He desired to honor God and his wife. He did not want to be the one who broke his marriage vows like so many other men he knew. He wanted to be the exception to the norm.

Later that evening when Dominic arrived home, Alexis was waiting for him. He was pleasantly surprised to learn his wife had taken off work to spend much-needed quality time with him. After putting his briefcase away, he walked into the kitchen to see what the tantalizing aroma was. On the stove, he found a roasting pan filled with tender baked chicken and oven-roasted potatoes. In a steamer, he saw fresh broccoli and carrots. In the oven, a fresh pan of cornbread was baking. Dominic's mouth began to water as he took in all the different aromas.

Standing behind him with her hand on her hip, Alexis watched her husband silently appreciate the work she had put in in the kitchen. When Dominic turned around, his eyes were moist. Alexis could see he was touched.

"Awe, babe. What's wrong?" she asked him.

"Oh, it's nothing. I was just thinking about how blessed I am to have you in my life."

"Thank you. I just wanted to take this evening off to show you how much I appreciate you. I know I have been out of touch for a while, but things are going to change around here."

"That sounds good to me," Dominic interjected. "What do you have in mind besides this wonderful dinner you have prepared?"

"Well, why don't you get cleaned up while the bread finishes baking, and I will tell you all about the weekend away I have planned for us over dinner."

Her words caused a lump to form in Dominic's throat. A weekend away usually meant extra time for intimacy between the two of them. But, with Dominic's extra-curricular activities earlier that day, Dominic knew having a moment of intimacy with his wife would not be a wise course of action for that weekend.

"What's the matter, honey?" she asked after seeing him grow slightly uncom-fortable.

"Nothing. I'm just surprised. I will take my shower and meet you at the table in about fifteen minutes," Dominic said before kissing his wife gently on her lips.

A few moments later in the shower, Dominic enjoyed the feeling of the warm water running down his body. Yet, he felt so unclean and was overwhelmed with guilt. As he reflected back on the incident when another woman had her hands and lips all over him and how he had entered inside of her, he was filled with grief and remorse. He began to cry out to God and plead for forgiveness. He wanted desperately to go back in time and undo what he had done. But, of course, he could not.

After Dominic finished praying and repenting of his wrongdoings, he looked up and realized he was still in the shower. He wasn't sure how much time had passed, but the water had grown cold, and he was on his knees. The Spirit of the Lord had engulfed him, and he had forgotten the time and the place of his existence. He felt good to be in the presence of the Lord.

After drying off and dressing in a fresh pair of pants and a shirt, Dominic met his wife at the dining room table. He stared upon her beauty without saying a word.

"Honey, what is it? Why are you looking at me that way?" Alexis inquired.

"I'm just admiring your beauty. Thank you for taking time from your busy schedule. This means a lot to me," Dominic responded.

"No problem, babe. Now, let me tell you about the weekend I have planned for us."

"I'm all ears," Dominic's mouth said, while his heart was yet apprehensive. He knew with the prayer he had just recently prayed, God had forgiven him, but he wasn't so sure his wife would feel the same way if he passed something to her from another woman. So, he was concerned about making love to her before ensuring he was as clean as he was before his escapade. He knew that would take a few weeks to find out. Hopefully, Alexis would not become suspicious if they did not make love during that time frame.

Time went on, and Dominic did not experience contracting any sexually transmitted diseases, nor did Kim end up pregnant. He broke off his communication with Kim after apologizing to her about his actions. He admitted to her that he was as much to blame as she was. It was a two-party act, and obviously he was a willing participant. However, he was no longer willing to participate in the act of infidelity. Kim said she understood his position, and she actually apologized for being the catalyst in their momentary affair.

Life as Dominic knew it went back to normal, with the exception of his wife making more time for him and his needs. Also, Dominic re-dedicated his life to God and the service he would render unto Him.

You may be utterly appalled by Dominic's actions as a married man. But, let me warn you- be careful about passing judgment because any one of us can find ourselves in a position that we never believed we would be in. Yes, many situations like Dominic's are calculated and are entered into and executed without remorse.

God knows the intent of our hearts. He knows if we have malicious intent, and He knows if we acted out of a need to fill a void in our lives. Am I saying our acts are okay if our intentions are pure? No, I am saying- God knows what leads us into certain situations.

However, He wants us to be strong and fight temptation. I Corinthians 10:13 says, *"There hath no temptation taken you but such as is common to man: but God is faithful, who will not suffer you to be tempted above that ye are able; but will with the temptation also make a way to escape, that ye may be able to bear it."* God knows we will be tempted; however, He does not want us to yield to the temptation and commit acts of sin. He wants us to flee.

Did Dominic have an opportunity to flee? Of course, he did. First of all, he shouldn't have been at Kim's home. Secondly, when she opened the door with not much on, he could have fled. Thirdly, after he entered and she lifted her leg up to expose herself to him, he could have fled. Fourthly, when she slid her leg across his lap, he could have pushed it aside and fled. Do you see the point here? There were many opportunities to escape the situation.

All in all, what is most important is Dominic did not stay in his sin. He repented and got his life back on track. This is what God wants us to do. He wants us to continue to move forward and to keep our eyes on the prize. Philippians 3:13-14 says, *"Brethren, I count not myself to have apprehended: but this one thing I do, forgetting those things which are behind, and reaching forth unto those things which are before, I press toward the mark for the prize of the high calling of God in Christ Jesus."*

Who Would Have Thought?

"Thou tellest my wanderings: put thou my tears into thy bottle: are they not in thy book?"

Psalm 56:8

Pastor Floyd and his lovely wife, First Lady Chanel, have been married for thirty years, and together they built a strong church that has a solid foundation. Building a church was not the easiest thing they had ever done, but through trials and tests and successes and failures, they have been successful in keeping the doors of the church open. Their members are faithful tithers, and Floyd and Chanel are responsible about proper appropriation of the funds. God has blessed them abundantly in ministry and in the way of family, and they are forever grateful.

Together, they raised several children and are now assisting in raising their twelve grandchildren by being godly examples before them and speaking God's continual blessings into their lives. After the death of one of their daughters and her husband in an automobile accident, three of their grandchildren went to live permanently with them.

On Sunday mornings, as Chanel sits in her chair in the pulpit, she scans the congregation. She looks to see which members are there, how many visitors are there, and which members are absent.

On one particular Sunday, as Chanel was scanning the congregation, her eyes landed on one of the male members. At that very moment, he looked in her direction, and their eyes locked. The glance they shared lasted a little longer than normal. Eventually, Chanel turned her eyes away, but she couldn't help to wonder what his extended gaze meant. She had never experienced that with him before. Other men in the congregation constantly stared her up and down, but she paid their glances no attention. She knew she was a very attractive woman, but she also knew to whom her heart belonged.

The young man, whose name is Donnie, with whom Chanel had locked eyes was about fifteen years her junior. He had been a member of their church for about ten years. When he first began attending the church, Chanel and Floyd both took an immediate liking to him. He was very helpful and always lent his skills and talents to the ministry. Above all, he loved the Lord and had dedicated his life to Him.

He rarely dated, but when he did, he focused on one woman at a time. When he learned the particular woman he was dating was not for him, he ended the relationship and moved on- back to his bachelor life he would go.

In the past, Donnie had been married, but the relationship ended after the birth of their second child. Although he is no longer married to his children's mother, he never allowed his failed marriage to get in the way of raising his children and his fatherly responsibilities. When his children were younger, he always had them with him, and they were as much members of the church as he was. Now, his children are young adults and are off in college. Donnie remains the proud dad and visits them whenever their schedules coincide.

On one Saturday afternoon years before, Donnie had walked into Chanel's office. He frequently dropped by the church in the evenings after work and on Saturdays, as he lived in the neighborhood. Sometimes, he would do 'odds-and-ends' jobs at the church to make sure everything was functioning properly. Because of his dedication to the church, Floyd referred to him as 'son' and had literally taken him under his wing as he filled the role of surrogate father. Floyd was about twenty-five years Donnie's senior.

On that Saturday, when Donnie reached Chanel's desk, he leaned down to greet her with a peck on the cheek. As he leaned in to softly kiss her cheek, she turned her face towards him and his kiss landed on her lips. Neither of them apologized, but at the same time they did not discuss it. They both went on as if it had never happened.

The week after the uncomfortable glance during the morning worship service, Donnie discovered he had not stopped thinking about Chanel. And he had to admit to himself his thoughts were not pure. He knew it was wrong to think of Chanel that way with her being a married woman and all, but his flesh was rising, and he just could not get her off his mind.

With his flesh getting the best of him, he picked up is his phone and dialed Chanel's cell phone number. To his surprise, she actually answered. After making pleasantries and small talk, Donnie decided to tell Chanel what had been on his mind for some time- even before the glance that past Sunday. Slowly and cautiously, he began to tell her how much he admired her and how beautiful he thought she was.

When he noticed how receptive she was to his compliments and how she began to give compliments of her own, he decided to go a step further. Donnie saw her compliments as an open door to speak freely to her, so he began to share with her dreams he had had of her.

At the end of his divulgement, the only thing Chanel could think to say was, "Whatever you dream about must be what's going on in your mind, or maybe it is one of your deepest desires."

"And so what if it is one of my deepest desires? What should I do about it?" Donnie asked boldly.

Chanel answered simply, "Do what's in your heart to do."

"I will do that."

After Donnie's final declaration, the two ended their conversation. However, they both sat still, in their respective locations, and they thought long and hard about the conversation they had just had. Donnie thought, *She is the first lady of our church. She is my pastor's wife.* Chanel thought, *I am married, and this man is one of our congregants.*

The next day when Donnie got off work, he made a point to stop by the church. He knew Chanel would be there working, just before her women's group. He hoped, however, no other women were present. He wanted a moment alone with Chanel. He wanted to see if the same vibe he felt over the phone would be present or if it were a figment of his imagination. Truth be told, his imagination could run wild, for it had a mind of its own.

When Donnie arrived to the church, to his disappointment, he did not see Chanel's car. His heart dropped. He decided to check the door to see if she was inside after all. There was a note posted on the door:

> Women's group is cancelled for tonight. We will meet at our regular time next week.
> Love,
> *Lady Chanel*

One week later, Donnie called Chanel on her cell phone while she was at the church office and asked if he could stop by and bring her lunch. She consented. On the way to the church, he stopped by a famous local restaurant that all the church members love to frequent and picked up her favorite menu items. He also stopped at Conroy's flowers and picked up a dozen red roses arranged in a beautiful vase.

When Donnie walked through the church doors, Chanel could smell the aroma of the food, and she knew he had brought her favorite dish from the restaurant- oxtails. Her mouth began to water and the butterflies in her stomach began to flutter even faster than they had already been fluttering as she felt the anticipation of seeing him rise.

When Donnie reached Chanel's office, he found her standing next to her desk waiting for him to enter. Her mouth opened widely when she saw the roses. She wasn't expecting anything of that magnitude. She was only anticipating lunch.

As Donnie placed the vase on Chanel's desk, Chanel grabbed his hand and pulled him close to her. She then lifted herself on her toes, so she could reach his lips. She quickly, but very sensually, placed a kiss on his lips. Donnie, being the take-charge type of guy that he is, received Chanel's invitation for intimacy. He placed his arms around her waist, with his hands firmly planted in the small of her back, drew her body close to his, and began to passionately kiss her. Chanel enjoyed his take-charge demeanor. She loved being with a man who knew what he wanted and went for it.

They continued to kiss until they heard the church door open a few minutes later. The unexpected guest's voice called out loudly, "First Lady Chanel, are you here? I saw your car outside."

Chanel with a weak and surprised voice answered, "Yes, I'm here. I'm in my office. Come on back."

Meanwhile, Donnie made himself comfortable in one of the chairs. A moment later, Sister Rosalyn Green walked into the office with a big smile on her face. She was a single lady and very flirtatious. She had flirted with Donnie from time to time over the past year and even hinted to him that she wanted him to take her out. But to put it quite frankly, she was not his type at all.

Donnie loved women with class, not those who threw themselves at men. He liked to be the pursuer. He did not like a woman to pursue him. Even though he was relatively young, he was old fashioned in that respect.

When Sister Green entered the office, the first two things she saw were the roses and Donnie. She spoke to Chanel and then she immediately walked over to Donnie, leaned over and gave him a tight embrace. Chanel watched her and gave Donnie a disapproving look while Sister Green had her back turned to her. Donnie smiled at Chanel while hugging Sister Green. His smile told her not to worry. Sister Green was no competition for her.

After hugging Donnie a little longer than necessary, Sister Green stood perfectly straight and walked over to Chanel's desk and began to admire the beautiful roses.

"Pastor Floyd is such the romantic," she commented. Chanel remained quiet.

"These roses are gorgeous," Sister Green continued.

"Yes, they are," Chanel agreed. "What brings you by Rosalyn?"

Feeling suddenly out of place, Rosalyn answered, "Oh, I stopped by to bring ticket money for the Women's Conference next weekend."

"Excellent," Chanel said with her hand extended. She desperately wanted to move the interruption along and get to her lunch and her afternoon with Donnie. Rosalyn noticed she was being hurried, so she handed the money over and apologized for her interruption of the meeting that was obviously taking place before she had entered.

"Don't worry about it," Chanel said. "We are just trying to take care of a little business. I'm sure you understand."

"Oh sure," Rosalyn said pouting a little.

"I'll see you at service early tomorrow morning," Donnie offered.

"You most certainly will," Rosalyn said with a big smile.

After Rosalyn left, Chanel sat in her chair and resumed her visit with Donnie. She began to open the bag that contained the food with the irresistible aroma. Moments later, Donnie and Chanel dined peacefully without any further interruptions. Neither of them really knew what to say, so they made small talk and enjoyed each other's company.

A few months later after several more lunches and dinners in Chanel's office or at Donnie's home, Donnie called Chanel and asked if she wanted to take a drive with him. She consented and asked how she should dress.

He responded, "Wear something comfortable and be sure to wear shoes you can walk in."

"Will do," she replied and disconnected the call.

The two of them met at a local park. Chanel parked her car and got into Donnie's car. He immediately got on the interstate and away they went. After an hour's drive, they found themselves driving up a steep road that led up to a mountaintop. Chanel enjoyed the scenery as they drove along.

Excited to be with each other, they held hands along the drive and constantly smiled at each other. When they arrived to their destination, Chanel noticed they were at a lodge. She felt the butterflies moving about anxiously in her stomach. She knew where the evening was heading, and she was nervous. She had never been with another man for all the years she had been married.

After Donnie checked into the lodge, he went back to the car and asked Chanel to go inside with him. As they walked down the corridor, their hearts beat rapidly. Both of them were very nervous, but excited. As Donnie opened the room door, he smiled at Chanel with his pretty white teeth. Secretly, she had always loved his smile and the dimple in his left cheek that seemed to be always begging her to kiss it. That day, she planned to do just that.

After getting settled into the room, they made themselves comfortable on the bed. Neither of them wanted to move too quickly. But as soon as their bodies touched, it was a done deal. At first, they only caressed each other and reminisced about how long they had known each other and how much they had secretly admired each other.

Chanel laid her head on Donnie's chest as she caressed his pecs. She loved that he was in such great shape. But being several years older than he was, she was concerned about what he would think of her body. To her surprise, he only had nice things to say.

After lying wrapped in each other's arms for an hour, Donnie finally made his move. He gently slid his body over on top of Chanel's while looking at her deeply in her eyes.

"Are you okay with this?" Donnie whispered. Chanel did not answer audibly. She only nodded her head, as she looked deeply into Donnie's eyes. For a moment, Donnie was frozen in his position, as he hovered over Chanel. He just kept staring at her. Then, slowly but surely, he lowered himself onto her and began to kiss her deeply. At the same time, he lifted up one of her legs and then the other.

As Chanel felt Donnie's every move, she knew the moment of their body's coming together was imminent. Then, she felt her body stiffen. Donnie stopped kissing her and placed his mouth by her ear. "Relax, sweetheart. I just want to love you."

At the sound of his voice, Chanel's body relaxed, and she felt him gently push his body inside of hers. She squealed with delight. The sensations she felt, she had never experienced before. She did not know such pleasure was possible. As her squeals grew louder and louder, Donnie covered her mouth with his to muffle the sounds, so they would not disturb anyone in the neighboring rooms. However, he did not stop pleasuring her. He had wanted her for so long that he dare not stop prematurely before he allowed her to reach a climax and before he reached one himself.

As the evening wore on, Donnie and Chanel continued to enjoy each other's company. They were acting like love-starved teenagers who had gone hungry for too long. They were happy to be with each other and did not want the moment to end.

A few hours later, the evening did come to an end. Donnie and Chanel found them-selves on the same highway descending the mountain. They drove until they reached Chanel's car. Donnie had planned for them to go to dinner, but when the dinner hour came, neither of them was hungry for food. They preferred to spend their time alone.

Donnie parked his car next to Chanel's and turned the engine off. Instead of him getting out to open her door, he just sat there continuing to hold his hand in hers.

She did not attempt to release her hand from his grasp. She just sat there quietly. Neither of them wanted their time together to end.

Finally, Donnie broke the silence. "You're mine now," he said, as he looked Chanel in her face.

"What do you mean by that?"

"I mean you belong to me now. It doesn't matter if you are married to Floyd or not, you are mine." Chanel actually felt the same way about him, but she remained quiet and watched Donnie's expression. She could tell he loved her, and she felt the same way about him. It was as though they had a secret passion for each other for a number of years, and one day it was surprisingly unleashed. They knew it was wrong, but they did not try to fight it.

The affair between Donnie and First Lady Chanel went on for a few years. The relationship finally ended when Donnie began dating someone he could have a true relationship with. After dating for a while, Donnie became engaged to be married. From that point forward, Donnie and Chanel ceased their intimate relationship.

Today, they remain close and are great friends. When they talk, the sparks continue to fly between them, but Donnie respects the covenant he has with his wife, even if Chanel did not choose to go that route when it came to being with him even though she had a husband.

As you read the story, I'm sure on the outset you did not see any remorse in either Chanel or Donnie. Maybe they were remorseful, and maybe they were not. Maybe they would have done something differently if they had an opportunity to do it over again, or maybe they would do the same thing all over again. Who knows?

What I do know is this- both Chanel and Donnie put an end to their relationship and repented before God. They could have continued seeing each other even after Donnie got married. But someone had to stand up for what was right. After Donnie made his stand, they both had an opportunity to get their lives right with God. Both have decided to be faithful stewards to God and to be faithful to their spouses.

I'll See You When We Get There!

"No one who is born of God will continue to sin, because God's seed remains in them; they cannot go on sinning, because they have been born of God."

I John 3:9 (NIV)

Jeffrey laid his head back on his seat as he sat on the 747 jet. As he looked out the window, he felt the plane begin to move and eventually his eyes witnessed the same. As the plane made is final pre-parations for take-off, Jeffrey felt his excitement increase. He was really looking forward to reaching his destination, as he was in much need of a vacation. For the last six months, he had put in long hours at work and could barely come up for air. But now, he was putting work behind him, and it was his time to relax.

This year, Jeffrey was vacationing in the Cayman Islands. But he would not be spending his fourteen-day vacation alone. Vanessa would be joining him as she always did.

It had been a few months since they had spent time alone together, for their situation was very precarious. They were both ministers of the gospel of Jesus Christ and single, even though they considered themselves to be in a committed relationship with one another. But, their jobs kept them from being together on a full-time basis, not to mention they lived in two different states. So once a year, they took a break from their everyday lives and routines, and they spent time away together.

Their sordid relationship all began ten years prior when they met at a gym. Each one was determined to keep his/her physique intact, so each one worked out four to five times a week. Both were obsessed with their physical appearance, and neither one of them was willing to allow it to diminish, so they worked hard at keeping every part of their body in shape.

One day, Vanessa was on the treadmill, and Jeffrey, who was visiting her city for business, walked over to the only available machine, which just so happened to be right next to hers. As she walked three miles on the treadmill, she had her earplugs in her ears, which were attached to her iPhone. As she was listening to Whitney Houston's Greatest Hits, she sang along to each song that played. Her voice matched Whitney's note for note. And, she hit every octave as she walked along on the treadmill, completely in tune to Whitney's rhythmic beats.

Vanessa was oblivious to anyone else who was there in the gym with her, but Jeffrey, as he walked five miles, took in the concert Vanessa was unknowingly giving him. He enjoyed the melody of her voice and made every fiber of his being moved like he had not felt it move in a long time.

When Vanessa was done with her three miles, she looked up as she removed the earplugs from her ears. She noticed Jeffrey watching her intently. She was not flattered at all by him watching her. Instead, she was put off and irritated. She had half a mind to ask him what he was looking at, but she decided against it. He was a stranger, and she did not want to open up a can of confrontation. So, she simply smiled.

When Jeffrey saw her smile, he felt compelled to ask her name. From there, they sparked up a conversation. That conversation led them into a relationship that has now been in existence for over three years.

After spending that initial weekend together, every few months Jeffrey and Vanessa get together for a weekend getaway. Then once a year, they choose a vacation spot and just relax and enjoy each other's company.

At the airport, Jeffrey and Vanessa met up after their respective flights. They embraced one another with love and concern. They both knew they desperately needed to talk. After getting the rental car and making their way to the hotel, they made plans to go out to dinner. Normally, the first thing they do is undress, caress each other, hold each other and make love.

That time things were different. Both of their minds were deep in thought, so they figured dinner should be the first course of action. Once they arrived to the restaurant and had selected their dinner choices from the menu, Jeffrey took Vanessa's hand in his and looked deeply into her eyes and said, "This talk is well overdue. We know we cannot continue to live our lives this way. We are not living by the Gospel that we preach. Our lives are not pleasing to God. No matter how much good we do, this one lifestyle choice has created such a bad stain on our entire character. I often wonder what my pastor would think if he knew that I was involved with another minister, and I wonder what your pastor would think if he knew that you were involved with me. But more importantly than what man thinks, we know that God is not pleased."

"Yes, Jeffrey. I know what you are saying is true, and I have given it a lot of thought lately as well. The way I see it, we have to choose between three options. We can either continue our relationship and live in sin, we can continue our relationship in a manner that will be pleasing to God and honorable before man, or we can stop seeing each other all together."

"Yes, I do realize that," Jeffrey said. "I have come to care for you deeply and love you. I have the utmost respect for you. Our situation is challenging with you living in one place and me living in another, but I do think it is time, actually past time, Vanessa to right our wrong. I want you to know that I am sincerely sorry for putting you in this situation and not honoring you how a man should honor a woman that he truly loves and respects."

Jeffrey paused for a minute, reached into his pocket, slid his chair back, kneeled down on one knee, right next to Vanessa's chair and opened a ring box right before her very eyes. Vanessa's hand moved to her mouth in utter surprise. She had not expected what was coming next, but she kept quiet and let Jeffrey say what he needed to say.

"Vanessa, I love you. I cherish you. It will be a great honor to me if you would take my hand in holy matrimony. Vanessa, will you be my wife?"

Jeffrey's unexpected proposal completely shocked Vanessa. She really didn't know what to say. She knew deep in her heart she loved Jeffrey also. But before she could answer his question, she needed to know the details. She needed to know if he was asking her to leave her home town and move to his, or if he was planning to leave his home town and move to hers, or if they would move somewhere else together. She needed answers before she could give him an answer.

So slowly and carefully, she said, "Jeffrey, I love you too, and I never thought that you would ask me that question. But, we really do need to talk."

Jeffrey looked into her eyes and slowly stood to his feet and sat back in his chair. "So, are you denying my request?" he asked hesitantly.

"No, Jeffrey. Not at all. I just need answers. We really do need to talk. Our situation is quite complicated."

Jeffrey said, "Well, let's uncomplicate it. I don't want to continue to live like this any longer."

"Yes, I understand, Jeffrey, but are you asking me to move to your home, or are you willing to give up your home and go to mine?"

Jeffrey understood her concern. "Well, Vanessa, I know you love your hometown and your family is there. I love my hometown as well, but I don't have any family, so I am willing to leave and move to your hometown. However, I will not be moving into your home. I will be purchasing a home for the two of us. How does that sound to you?"

Vanessa jumped out of her chair screaming with joy. She ran over to

Jeffrey's chair, placed her arms around his neck, and squeezed him tightly. All she could say was, "Yes, Jeffrey. I will marry you."

Jeffrey and Vanessa's story is not uncommon. Members of the body of Christ have been committing fornication and adultery for centuries and continue to do so even in today's societies. Furthermore, the mindset people have when they engage in these sexual sins is also not uncommon because the associated thoughts that accompany these behaviors have become so commonplace.

What is admirable though and honorable before God is when man can admit his wrongdoings and turn from his evil ways.

"If my people, which are called by my name, shall humble themselves, and pray, and seek my face, and turn from their wicked ways; then will I hear from heaven, and will forgive their sin, and will heal their land" II Chronicles 2:14.

God is not impressed by those who choose to go along with the status quo. What impresses Him is those who stand for what is holy. God desires holiness from His children. He tells us this in I Peter 1:16, *"Because it is written, Be ye holy; for I am holy."*

When Jeffrey decided to break the cycle of fornication between himself and Vanessa, he made a stand for holiness and righteous living. He decided to put his selfish desires of remaining in his dwelling place aside and do what would be honorable for a man who carries the gospel of his lord and savior.

Neither he nor Vanessa wanted to be hypocritical in their walk with God. They wanted to be a sweet-smelling savor unto the Lord's nostrils.

After marrying and relocating, Jeffrey and his new bride had a marriage that could and would receive God's blessings. Ecclesiastes 4:12 says, *"And if one prevail against him, two shall withstand him; and a threefold cord is not quickly broken."* When a man and woman are bound in holy matrimony and their union is according to God's will, the verse in Ecclesiastes is applicable. The three-fold cord refers to the husband, the wife, and Jesus Christ.

Jesus becomes an avid supporter of that marriage and fights for it against the fiery darts of the enemy that will undoubtedly come.

If you are engaged in a romantic affair that is not with someone to whom you are married, you must make a decision like Jeffrey and Vanessa did. Until then, God will not be pleased, nor will He be glorified.

I Have Fallen

Enough is Enough!

"The heart is deceitful above all things, and desperately wicked: who can know it?"

Jeremiah 17:9

Marcus and Anaya have been dating for four years. They love each other dearly and find themselves to be completely in sync with one another. For the last two years, Marcus has been bringing up the topic of marriage, but Anaya is young and carefree and never settled in on taking Marcus's conversations regarding marriage seriously. To compound the matter, from time to time, she impulsively steps out on Marcus and dates other guys. Marcus had no knowledge about her affairs until one particular situation became volatile. Actually, it became dangerous for *both* Anaya and Marcus.

One night, Anaya stayed over Marcus's house. Early the next morning, Anaya was walking out to her car, so she could make her way to work. Halfway to her car, she turned around to wave goodbye to Marcus, who was in his upstairs bedroom window.

All of a sudden, Anaya let out a very loud scream. She was horrified at what her eyes were showing her. Marcus ran down the stairs and out the front door. He immediately looked over to see what had caught Anaya's attention and caused her reaction. When he lifted his eyes, he was just as horrified. Spray painted on the side of his house were the words, "She is a whore!"

"What the hell is this?" Marcus belted out, not really expecting an answer from anyone.

"Oh, my God," was all Anaya could manage to say. Marcus walked over and ran his hand across the letters to see if the paint was still fresh. He wanted to get an idea of how long the astonishing words had been there.

"I'm calling the police," Anaya said.

"Listen, you need to get to work. I will call them in a minute," Marcus interjected.

He then proceeded to take Anaya by her hand and walk her over to her car. Upon their arrival to the driver side door, Anaya once again let out a piercing scream. Marcus looked down and saw a very long scrape along the side of Anaya's car. Someone had purposefully run his key along the side of her shiny black car.

They continued to survey the car to see if there was any further damage. They found her two back tires slashed. Anaya immediately pulled out her cell phone and began to call the police. When the police arrived, they made a report and asked a series of questions in an effort to ascertain whom the vandal was.

The police asked Anaya and Marcus, "Does either of you know who could have done this and why your home and car have been targeted?"

They could not think of who could possibly dislike them that much that they would wish harm to their personal property, but as the day wore on, Anaya would find out exactly who the culprit was and why she was the target of such mistreatment.

After Anaya spoke with the police and the report had been filled out, she and Marcus got into his car. He drove her to work, so she would not be late. On the way there, both of their minds were racing around the track trying to determine who could have possibly done that to them.

Anaya thought about Marcus's ex-girl-friends. In the past, she had had a couple of run ins with them. Marcus was thinking the same thing. He knew he had broken some hearts when he settled down to singly date

Anaya. But that was years ago. There was no reason for anyone to lash out now.

When Anaya arrived to work, neither she nor Marcus was anxious for her to leave him. But, duty called. Anaya was the manager of her floor at the office where she worked. She would be irresponsible if she called in without there being a serious emergency.

Anaya was deeply disturbed as she went through her work day. She kept wondering and wondering who could have targeted Marcus's home and her car. As she sat at her desk, she found herself distracted.

Before lunch, Marcus called Anaya to see if she wanted him to pick her up for lunch or if she wanted him to bring something to her. She declined his offer because she wanted him to enjoy his day off. After all, he did have to pick her up afterward, so they could get tires for her car. So, she didn't want him to go out of his way to drive over there three times in one day.

Just as Anaya ended her phone call with Marcus, one of her male co-workers walked into her office and asked if she wanted to ride to a local restaurant to pick up lunch. She gladly accepted his invitation. Although she was distracted from work, her stomach had been talking to her for the last hour. When Anaya returned from picking up lunch, she walked to the staff break room and spread her lunch on the table.

Just as she was ready to dig in, her cell phone rang. She thought about ignoring it because she really wanted to bite into her pastrami sandwich. But, she chose to answer it anyway. However, she was not expecting the voice that was on the other end of the phone.

"Hello," she answered.

"Who was that you were riding with in the car a few minutes ago?" the voice asked. Before answering, Anaya quickly moved the phone from her ear and looked at it to check the caller ID. The caller ID read 'Restricted.'

"Who is this?" Anaya asked impatiently.

"Whose car were you in?" the voice asked.

"If you don't tell me who this is, I'm not answering your question," she stated firmly.

"Don't play dumb. You know who this is."

After the caller made the last statement, Anaya had a very good idea who was calling her and demanding answers. She took a deep breath and yelled into the phone, "Deondre, why are you calling me? I told you three months ago we were through!"

"Oh, you think you can decide when to pick me up and when to drop me? I decide when we are through. And, we are not through by a long shot!"

"Look, Deondre, as I explained before, we are not right for each other. I have a boyfriend."

"Yeah, you had a boyfriend when you were coming over to my house, but I didn't hear you mentioning him then."

"Deondre, what do you want?"

"I want to know who you were with in the car a few minutes ago."

"That was Matthew my co-worker. Why?"

"Is he your new victim?"

"I'm hanging up now," Anaya said as she disconnected from the call. She was completely irritated- more with herself for getting involved with Deondre in the first place and for being completely disloyal to Marcus who was totally unsuspecting.

After Anaya hung up, her phone rang again a minute later, and the caller ID showed 'Restricted' again. That time, she ignored the call. Actually, she removed her phone from the table and placed it in her purse. Then, she enjoyed her lunch.

Once Anaya finished her lunch, she made her way back to her office. However, she still could not concentrate on getting any work done. She was now less focused than before, after Deondre's call.

When she arrived back to her office, she closed her door, turned off her light and placed her head on her desk. Before long, she had fallen into a light sleep. She was awakened by the sound of her office phone ringing.

"Hello," Anaya answered sleepily.

"Babe," a voice said.

"Yes?" Anaya answered.

"Why aren't you answering your cell phone?"

"Oh, I think it's in my purse. What time is it?"

"It's ten minutes after four. Are you coming downstairs?"

"Oh yeah, Marcus. I'm coming right now."

"Why do you sound like you have been asleep?" he asked before hanging up.

"Because I was. I couldn't work with everything that happened this morning. I just laid my head on my desk. I didn't expect to fall asleep. I'll be right down. Okay?"

"Okay, babe."

After Anaya took the elevator down to the bottom floor, Marcus was standing there waiting for her with a bouquet of flowers. Anaya smiled for the first time that day since the early morning. Just as she reached for the flowers, another hand reached from behind Marcus and grabbed the flowers first.

"I'll take those," Deondre said as he snatched the flowers from Marcus's grasp. "I don't think I appreciate you giving flowers to my girl."

Both Anaya and Marcus stood there with their mouths agape. Then, Marcus broke the silence.

"Who is this clown, Anaya?"

"I'm Deondre. That's who I am. Who the hell are you?" Deondre said as he threw the flowers on the floor.

Anaya reached down to pick up the flowers, and Deondre pushed her back to prevent her from retrieving them. Marcus grabbed Deondre, lifting him off the floor, and threw him across the room. At that moment, a security officer walked over and demanded to know what was going on. Everyone began to talk at once.

"One person at a time. Please!" the officer yelled. "Ma'am, why don't you tell me what is going on?"

"This man," she said pointing to Deondre, "is here without an invitation. I work here in the building, and I was just getting off work. My boyfriend came to pick me up."

"Yes, I have seen you around," the officer said while nodding his head. "Okay, I'm going to have to ask you to leave the building, sir," he said to Deondre.

Deondre reluctantly started walking toward the door, as he did not want to cause any problems for himself by remaining on the premises. When he reached the front door, he turned and said, "Hey, man. You should know- she's nothing but a whore!"

Marcus immediately looked at Anaya with an accusing look on his face. He remembered the very words that were painted on the side of his home. At that moment, they both realized who the vandal was that had been there the night before defacing their property.

Anaya began to cry and profusely apologize to Marcus. But all Marcus said was, "Let's go!" Anaya followed him to the car crying all the way, as she held the broken flowers in one hand.

On the drive home, Marcus did not utter a word, and all Anaya could do was cry. She knew she had heart him deeply. She knew that he was acutely aware that she had stepped out on him, and it was because of her actions they were being attacked at that time.

Marcus drove directly to his home where Vanessa's car was parked. While she was at work, he had called a tire service professional and had the two tires replaced. She thought they were going to do it after work, but he wanted to surprise her. When she saw what he had done, she cried even harder.

After exiting Marcus's vehicle, they went into his house. "Is he the reason you don't want to get married?" Marcus asked.

"Of course not!" Anaya yelled.

"But you've been sleeping with him."

"Yes, I slept with him, but I broke it off a little while ago. I haven't been seeing anyone but you."

"Oh, is that supposed to make me feel better?"

"No. I'm just trying to explain that I did mess up, but after that I have been faithful to you."

"Okay, that may be true. But I was thinking while you were gone. I was wondering why things were happening to us- not just today- but the arguments we have and all that goes along with them. I figured it was because we are not living a life that God is pleased with, and that makes us open targets for the enemy."

"Marcus, that makes a lot of sense. So, what are you suggesting?"

"Well, we can either get married like I had suggested before or we can go our separate ways. I am not willing to live like this anymore. It is not worth the risks we are taking."

"Well, I don't know if it's that simple."

"Yes, it is that simple. We need to make a choice. And, since it is so difficult for you, I guess I will make the final decision. We need to go our separate ways."

"Oh, is it that easy for you to break up with me?" Anaya said, with the water works starting up again.

"No, it isn't. I love you dearly, but I can see that the love I have for you is not the same love you have for me. I learned that today when what's his name showed up at your job. Breaking up with you is not easy, but it is necessary. God will carry me through this," Marcus stated as he sat down on the couch emotionally exhausted.

Anaya could hear in Marcus's voice that he was very hurt, and she understood why he needed to do what he was doing. There was really nothing she could say. She knew she wasn't ready for marriage, so she had to respect his wishes.

Marcus and Anaya did indeed go their separate ways. Marcus was certain that he wanted to get his life back on track and serve God honestly and faithfully, and living a life that included fornication was not pleasing to God.

Anaya, on the other hand, is still up to her same mode of operation. She is not as dedicated to God as Marcus is. She loves God, but she has not completely dedicated her life to Him. She wants to walk in her free will and do just as her flesh pleases.

Like Marcus, each of us must take a stand for righteousness. We cannot be led by our flesh, like Anaya, doing any and everything that we will to do. If we live by our fleshly desires, we will die by those same desires.

Matthew 5:6 says, *"Blessed are they which do hunger and thirst after righteousness: for they shall be filled."*

What desires are leading the choices you are making? Are you being led by the spirit of God, or are you being led by your own spirit that is operating contrary to the will of God?

In the end, God will have the final say so. Philippians 2:10-11 say, *"That at the name of Jesus every knee should bow, of things in heaven, and things in earth, and things under the earth; And that every tongue should confess that Jesus Christ is Lord, to the glory of God the Father."*

Whatever we do in this life, we will have to answer for it in the next. And the answer will be given at the judgment seat of Christ.

Final Thoughts

It is easy to point the finger at, ridicule, and pass judgment on those who have fallen short of God's expectations of His children. However, the Bible warns us against sitting in the seat of the scornful. A scorner is one who looks upon another with contempt or disdain and sees that person as unworthy or despicable.

Psalm 1:1 states, *"Blessed is the man that walketh not in the counsel of the ungodly, nor standeth in the way of sinners, nor sitteth in the seat of the scornful."*

We would be wise to issue compassion to others instead of scorn. Through compassion, we are able to lend a helping hand through prayer or whatever method is possible to draw our brother or our sister back to God and out of the snare of the enemy.

The enemy desires to entrap and ensnare us. He does not want us to receive the favor or rewards of the Lord. He wants us to suffer the same destiny to which he is doomed.

What is your choice today? Will you reach down to your fallen brother or sister and pull him/her up, or will you be the one to ostracize him/her and make him/her an outcast? God has given us free will. What is your will today as it concerns your brother or sister in Christ?

Gift of Salvation

for Non-Believers

"For all have sinned, and come short of the glory of God."
Romans 3:23

This section was written especially for non-believers, those who have not accepted the gift of salvation. The gift of salvation saves souls from eternal damnation and is a free gift offered by God himself.

John 3:16-18 says, *"For God so loved the world, that he gave his only begotten Son, that whosoever believeth in him should not perish, but have everlasting life. For God sent not his Son into the world to condemn the world; but that the world through him might be saved. He that believeth on him is not condemned: but he that believeth not is condemned already, because he hath not believed in the name of the only begotten Son of God.*"

This section of scripture tells us God's purpose for giving His son Jesus to the world. The world was in a bad condition. The world was overwrought with sin; the people were living for fleshly desires rather than for God's desires.

As a result of the world's conditions, God decided that He would offer the perfect sacrifice that would save the world from being a place where people were lost and had no hope. He decided that His own son could stand in proxy for the sin-filled world, taking all sin upon Himself.

So Jesus came, born of a virgin, to save this dying world. He walked on this earth for 33 ½ years, doing the work of His Heavenly Father. At the appointed time, He died by way of crucifixion upon a cross at

Calvary, on Golgatha's hill. He shed his blood and died for you and for me. Because His blood was pure, it paid the penalty for all unrighteousness and gave those who believe in Him direct access to His father's throne.

Scripture tells us in Matthew 27:51 that the veil of the temple was ripped in two from top to bottom, at the moment that Jesus' spirit left His body. As a result of the veil's removal, we are no longer required to have a high priest make intercession for us. We, as the children of the Most High God, are able to approach the throne God for ourselves, and Jesus sits on the right hand of the Father making intercession for us.

But what is even more miraculous than God offering His own son as the perfect sacrifice was the fact that when Jesus was placed in grave clothes and placed in a tomb, He only remained there until the third day. God would not have it that His son would remain in the heart of the earth forever. In order for people to believe in the awesome power of God and His dear son Jesus, a miracle had to be performed. So, on the third day, after Jesus died on the cross, He was resurrected, demonstrating the omnipotence of God. This very act was the act that would cause people to believe in a god that reigns supreme and holds the power of the universe in His very hands, a god that could save them from themselves.

Today, if you are an unbeliever, you can change your destiny. You can change where you will spend your eternity. Our Heavenly Father gives us the freedom of choice about how we want to live our life here on earth and how we want to spend eternity. In Deuteronomy 30:19, God boldly declares, *"I call heaven and earth to record this day against you, that I have set before*

*you life and death, blessing and cursing:
therefore choose life, that both thou and
thy seed may live."*

So, dear friend what choice will you
make today? Will you spend your eternity
with the Creator or will you suffer Hell's
eternal flames? Again, the choice is yours.
Just as the men aboard the ship who were
with Jonah became believers, you too can
make a choice to accept the only one and
true living God as your god.

If after reading the above passages, you
have decided that you want to spend your
eternity in Heaven with God, the creator,
and His son Jesus, and the Holy Spirit, read
through what has affectionately come to be
known as the Roman's Road. This is the
road to salvation. As you read through the
scriptures that comprise the Roman's Road,
you will also read the explanation for each

scripture so you will have clarity about what you are reading and confessing.

The Roman's Road to Salvation

The road to salvation begins with Romans 3:23 which declares, *"For all have sinned, and come short of the glory of God."* This scripture explains that everyone has come short of God's glory and needs redemption. Then Romans 6:23a states, *"For the wages of sin is death."* Here, we learn that the consequence of living a life of sin is death. Everyone will experience physical death as a result of the sin committed in the garden of Eden, but those who commit themselves to a life of sin will suffer eternal damnation in the lake of fire (Rev. 19).

Continue with the rest of verse 6:23 that says, *"but the gift of God is eternal life through Jesus Christ our Lord."* There is an alternative to suffering eternal damnation. We can accept the gift of salvation by accepting Jesus as our personal lord and savior. Then, Romans 5:8 says, *"But God commendeth his love toward us, in that, while we were yet sinners, Christ died for us."* We are able to receive the gift of salvation because Christ came to earth and shed His blood for us on the cross.

Continue to Romans 10: 9-10 which says, *"That if thou shalt confess with thy mouth the Lord Jesus, and shalt believe in thine heart that God hath raised him from the dead, thou shalt be saved. For with the heart man believeth unto righteousness; and with the mouth confession is made unto salvation."* If we confess with our mouths that Jesus is the son of God, that he came and died for our sins, and that God raised Him from the dead, we will receive salvation.

Finish with Romans 10:13, which states, *"For whosoever shall call upon the name of the Lord shall be saved."* Call upon the name of God by saying these words, **"Lord Jesus, come into my heart and save me Lord. I believe that you are the Son of God who came and died on the cross for my sins. I believe that you rose from the grave. I also believe that you now sit in heaven on the right side of the Father, making intersession for me. I accept you as my Lord and my Savior.**"

Now that you have confessed with your mouth that Jesus is the son of God and that He died for our sins and rose from the grave, **YOU ARE NOW SAVED!!!!** You will spend your eternity in heaven.

The next step is very important- you must find a bible-based church that teaches the word of God and confesses the Lord Jesus Christ to be the son of God. Don't delay. Do this immediately. Do not leave yourself open to the enemy. Get connected with the saints of the Most High God and keep yourself covered with the unspotted blood of the lamb.

Here is my prayer for you.

Father God,

I thank you for the opportunity to minister your word to the unsaved, the unchurched, and the uncommitted. Father God, I pray now for the souls who have just received the gift of salvation. Lord Father, they have opened their hearts to you, and I know that you have received them into your kingdom and written their names in the Book of Life. Father God, I pray that you will touch their lives and show yourself mightily before them. Let their eyes be opened by the scales falling off, allowing them to see clearly.

Father God, I even pray for the backslider, those who have turned away from you after receiving the gift of salvation. You said in your word that you desire that none would perish. So Lord, I send your word to them right now praying that they would confess the iniquity in their heart, repent, and turn from their evil ways, so that they may receive a life of abundance. You said in your word in Matthew Chapter 14, that every knee shall bow before you and every tongue will confess that Jesus is Lord.

Father God, I pray now that we all come under subjection to your word and that we will humbly submit our lives to you. I ask all these things in the name of my Lord and Savior Jesus Christ.
Amen, Amen, Amen!!!!

I will continue to pray for your success in your walk with God. Remember, this spiritual walk that you are about to embark on will not be an easy walk, but remember, the race is not given to the swift but to those who endure to the end.

Be blessed with heaven's best. I love you!

ABOUT THE AUTHOR

Dr. Cassundra White-Elliott resides in California with her family, where as an English/Education professor she teaches at various community colleges and universities.

When writing, she writes with the direction of the Holy Spirit, in an effort to share with God's people all that He has for them.

In addition to teaching and writing, Dr. White-Elliott also serves as an evangelistic teacher. She is also the founder of International Women's Commission, a ministry that serves the needs of the entire person, by attending to healing the mind, body, soul, and spirit.

Dr. White-Elliott holds a Ph.D. in Education, a Master's in English Composition, and a Bachelor's in Education.

Dr. White-Elliott is also the founder of CLF Publishing, LLC. For your publishing needs, go online to www.clfpublishing.org.

OTHER BOOKS

BY THE AUTHOR

(All books can be purchased at

www.creativemindsbookstore or

amazon.com)

I Have Fallen

From Despair, through Determination, to Victory!

A lot can happen during a span of 40 years. The life of Dr. Cassundra White-Elliott has been anything but uneventful. From a fun-loving childhood sprinkled with incidents of abuse to a tumultuous young adulthood to a stable, secure adult life, she has experienced a full life, with much more to come. Her story is inspiring and motivating.

If anyone lacks hope, reading Dr. White-Elliott's autobiography will propel him/her into an attitude of "Maybe I can." This attitude, if nurtured and developed, will grow into an attitude of "Yes, I can." Throughout her life, Cassundra has always held in her heart the belief that she could achieve anything that she had a made-up mind to embark upon. She was determined to achieve her heart's desires, doing what God has called her to do. She takes no credit for herself. All the glory goes to God, for He is her driving force. In Him, she lives, moves, and has her being.

Through the Storm

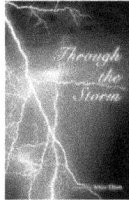

Through the Storm was duly inspired by the avaricious cloud of depression that decided to hover overhead of my daily existence in the latter part of 2007. Although I found it extremely difficult, I was once again compelled to not be defeated by just another snare that the enemy, the trickster, set for me. Once again, or more appropriately I should say *continuously*, he has exerted pernicious efforts to snatch the very life out of me by causing me to wallow in despair and to believe that I had been overcome by failure when in actuality and all reality, I was just experiencing a temporary setback. During those cloudy days, I had to remind myself daily that even though I was a target of the enemy, I am and will always be a child of the Most High god, Jehovah, who is my rock, my stability.

Unleashed Anger, Anger Unleashed

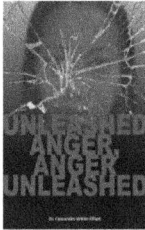

Introduction

What Is This Book All About?

As I prepared to embark upon the adventure of writing this book, I had to prepare myself to also be transparent. I have found that being transparent is required in order for healing to transpire, healing for all those that peruse the pages of this book and myself. And I may as well tell you that today, at the onset of this project, I have not been totally delivered from my condition of being an anger-filled person. However, I am definitely a work in progress. I have made strides with the assistance of my Lord and Savior, Jesus Christ, who is the head of my life. Without his love, guidance, and teachings, I would not be the woman of God I am today. I shudder to think where I could be instead and will therefore not entertain the thought.

Public Speaking in the Spiritual Arena

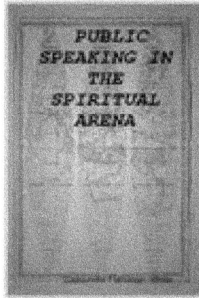

Gain the tools to speak successfully in public, with particular focus on the spiritual arena.

Where is Your Joppa?

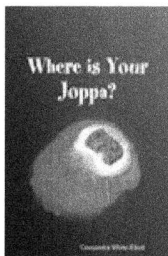

Where is Your Joppa? was written for the express purpose of illustrating God's call for obedience in the lives of believers with respect to the individual call that He has on each of our lives. As you read throughout the various chapters, notice that the emphasis is placed on our persistent disobedience in answering God's call in a specific area of our lives. We have become a people who are similar to the Israelites when they found themselves in the middle of the wilderness, following their exodus from Egypt. Before God, they murmured and complained about their current life conditions and failed to be obedient to God's statutes delivered through His servant Moses. Their persistent disobedience caused them to lose the opportunity to see and enter the Promised Land. I ask you, "What has your disobedience cost you?" "Was your disobedience worth what it cost you?"

Mayhem in the Hamptons

Romero and Yolanda optimistically plan for the day that is going to change their lives from being single persons to a couple who is united in holy matrimony. They, along with their parents, close friends and family, fly over to the infamous Hamptons, where only the rich and famous vacation, to have their dream wedding at the five-star Hampton Suites located on a peninsula in the Hamptons. Little do they know that their perfect day will turn out to be less than perfect when their wedding planner Mariesha Coleman suddenly goes missing!

Mayhem in the Hamptons is a tale that shares how the horrors of a woman's past can come back to haunt her in more than one way and the impact it can have on anyone who gets in the way.

The Preacher's Daughter

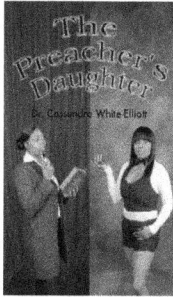

Tinisha, the daughter of a preacher, is a twenty-six year old God-fearing young woman endeavoring to complete law school so that she can make her mark in the courtroom. Working in one of the late-night clubs in Hollywood to earn money to pay her own way through school, Tinisha soon learns that life doesn't always go as planned. Finding her strength in her faith, Tinisha constantly finds herself praying as she watches God move miraculously in her life.

Preacher's Son

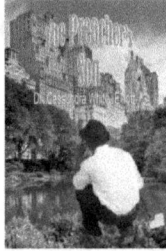

Romero Turner is a private investigator with a promising future. As he continues to build his career, he is excited about the cases he undertakes. However, his father Pastor Theodore Turner has other plans for his son's life. In the midst of trying to save his client's husband from Sylvester Domingo, a ruthless crime lord, Romero must try to salvage his relationship with his father. He must decide if ministry or life as a detective is in his future.

Lord, Teach Me to be a Blessing!

Lord, Teach Me to be a Blessing! will change a person's mentality from being centered around "me, myself, and I" to focusing on "others." The world system teaches us that it is acceptable to place ourselves above others in an attempt to get ahead and even to survive. Herbert Spencer coined the phrase *'survival of the fittest'* after reading Charles Darwin's theory of evolution. This concept of surpassing and outdoing others is the world's philosophy. However, the word of God does not subscribe to or promote this self-centered ideology, and therefore, neither should believers. We must hold fast to the truths outlined in Holy Scripture: *"Love thy neighbor as you love thyself"* (James 2:8) and *"It is more blessed to give than to receive"* (Acts 20:35).

While holding God's truths to be self-evident, we must demonstrate them to others, thereby showing them the way of the Lord of how to be a blessing to someone *rather* than looking to receive a blessing.

After the Dust Settles

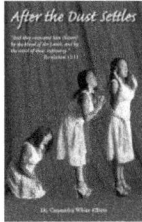

Throughout the journey of life, we all experience ups and downs and joys and pains. Most of us successfully find solutions to the situations/problems we encounter, but we often avoid dealing with the attached emotions. If we continue to ignore the emotions of pain, hurt, disappointment, anger, etc., we set ourselves up for destruction. Our families, our cultures, and our society tell us to be strong, to keep our chin up, and to grin and bear it. However, these methods of avoidance can lead us to strokes due to the undue amount of pressure we place on ourselves and/or mental illness from being unable to cope with the emotional baggage we have accumulated.

In *After the Dust Settles,* Dr. C. White-Elliott shares several situations that we all may encounter at one time or another in our lifetime and how to successfully navigate through them, so we can find ourselves emotionally healthy after the dust has settled and the situation has been rectified.

A Diamond in the Rough

A Diamond in the Rough Architecture Firm was built and is owned and operated by lead architect Kyra Fraser. For the last five years, Kyra has been extremely successful in business, but her love life leaves much to be desired.

Kyra has set high standards for herself and does not wish to take a man in any condition and attempt to make him over. She is looking for someone who is drama free, well educated, very cultured, fun-loving, good looking, self-motivated, and the list goes on.

Will Kyra find the man of her dreams, or will her dream just continue to be a dream?

As you delve into this page-turning novel, Kyra's reality will unfold as you are drawn into her world of design, love and office drama-which includes her best friend's husband who is looking for love in all the wrong places.

365 Days of Encouragement

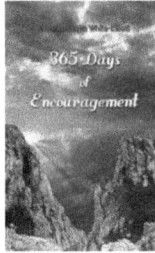

Just as our brain requires oxygen obtained from the air we breathe to sustain our mortal bodies, our spirit requires revitalization and encouragement in order to be strengthened each and every day of our lives. The revitalization and encouragement needed for the spirit of man comes directly from the word of God and assists us in walking according to the way of our heavenly Father. *365 Days of Encouragement* provides a scripture a day for each day of the year. Along with the daily scripture is a brief note of commentary also for the benefit of edifying the saints of God. It is my prayer that the people of God would live a fulfilled life through Christ Jesus. Knowing His word and understanding we can walk in the fulfillment thereof is empowering. We are instructed in II Timothy 2:15, "Study to shew thyself approved unto God, a workman that needeth not to be ashamed, rightly dividing the word of truth" (KJV).

A Mother's Heart

A Mother's Heart shares the unconditional love of mothers through a compilation of testimonies. Each testimony serves as a tribute to a special mother. The children of the represented mothers have lovingly written about their childhood, young adult life and/or older adult experiences they shared with their mother. As you read the writers' reflections, you will feel the expressions of love exude from the pages.

The purpose of this book is two-fold. First, it honors those mothers who stood by their children through the trials of life and showered them with unconditional love. Second, the book is a source of encouragement for mothers who may feel inadequate and question whether or not they are actually suited for motherhood.

Mothers may not be perfect, but they are definitely unmatched by any other category of person on God's green earth!

www.ingramcontent.com/pod-product-compliance
Lightning Source LLC
Chambersburg PA
CBHW061741020426
42331CB00006B/1322